TESSA RANSFORD (www.wisdomfield.com) is an established poet, translator, literary editor, and has worked as a cultural activist on many fronts over the last forty years. She founded and was the first director of the Scottish Poetry Library.

Tessa initiated the annual Callum Macdonald Memorial Award for publishers of pamphlet poetry in Scotland, now in its twelfth year, with the attendant fairs and website: www.scottish-pamphlet-poetry.com. She has had Royal Literary Fund fellowships at the Centre for Human Ecology and Queen Margaret University. She was president of Scottish PEN from 2003–6.

Tessa's *Not Just Moonshine, New and Selected Poems* was published in 2008 by Luath Press, Edinburgh and a new book of poems: *A Rug of a Thousand Colours*, in 2012.

The Urdu calligraphy in this book was created by artist Jila Peacock, jila@peacock.co.uk

don't mention this to anyone

Poems and prose fragments of life in the Punjab

TESSA RANSFORD

with calligraphy by
JILA PEACOCK

Luath Press Limited
EDINBURGH
www.luath.co.uk

Contents

Acknowledgements

THE MODEL SENTENCE sequence is published here in print for the first time. A number of poems in this collection have previously appeared, most recently in the following publications:

The Gift of Words, 2009 – an illustrated anthology in support of
  The Sick Kids Friends Foundation
Departures and Arrivals, 2009, CD published by Scottish PEN
Not Just Moonshine, Luath Press, 2008
Scottish Review of Books, Vol 3, No 4, 2007
Indian Selection, Akros Publications, 2000

I gratefully acknowledge the inspiration, help or encouragement of the following people in the making of this book:

> my late parents, Torfrida and Alister Ransford, the late Iain Kay
> Stiven, my children, my missionary and Pakistani colleagues, the
> late Duncan Glen, Sudeep Sen, Fiona Graham, Michael Lister,
> Gavin Macdougall and staff at Luath Press and of course my
> wonderfully talented friend, Jila Peacock.

As the poems look back on life and forebears, I dedicate them to the future in my eight grandchildren.

Foreword

TESSA RANSFORD'S Indian poems link us with a world now lost to most people, though not to the poet. This other world is a cosmos of sensations and spiritual perceptions that is vividly alive to her. It is also a characterful world in which religion and cultures mix in local communities and through specific relationships. To be British and Indian is a powerful though now often forgotten inheritance. These poems uncover and celebrate an 'Indian self'.

Moreover, as Ransford travels back in time, and sometimes space, the strangeness of 'then' encounters the difference of 'now'. The chance rediscovery of a set of cards with Urdu sentences for language lessons is the catalyst for recollection, and through this volume we are all invited on the journey.

Tessa Ransford has been a distinctive voice in Scottish poetry for nearly four decades. By refusing to conform to literary fashion, or gendered preconceptions, she has enriched the poetic ecology. These Indian sequences, gathered together here for the first time, reveal one important source of this poet's vision. Here are memories and experiences which move between life, art and social expectation with stubborn honesty, while interweaving influences that are formative in this writer's extensive body of poetic work.

If you have not previously encountered Tessa Ransford's poetry, then begin here. If you are already acquainted, then refresh your appreciation by dipping into this source, as if into a clear well of water.

Dr Donald Smith
Director
The Scottish Storytelling Centre

Introduction

THE POEMS HERE explore my connections with India and Pakistan. The first sequence is based on 'model sentences' which I used for learning Urdu when I first went to live in what was West Pakistan in January 1960 as a missionary's wife to work in women and children's welfare. The other poems in this collection were written at various times, and move between my childhood in India, which was still under the British Raj during the war years, and my later work in Pakistan. The rest of the poems were written in 2008, when I attended the Delhi International Literary Festival.

During the first eighteen months of our first five-year tour to Pakistan we worked intensively on learning to speak Urdu and Punjabi fluently. Part of this process involved memorising hundreds of model sentences which we wrote on cards, English on one side and Urdu on the other, in Persian script with a bamboo quill. Looking at this yellowing pack of cards recently, I chose a few of the model sentences as starters for poems.

Because many male missionaries went abroad unmarried, and then married women who were themselves already missionaries, wives who were not first missionaries in their own right were slightly suspect. As a result, some of us felt we had to prove ourselves by working hard, not complaining or suggesting better ways of doing things and generally by showing ourselves to be what was described as 'spiritually strong'.

Looking back on those times, we could of course never return to the India of our childhood, but in a sense I did, through living in Pakistan and bringing up my own first three children who were born there: one in Sialkot in the Punjab, one in Murree in the hills north of Rawalpindi, and one in Karachi. Those of us born in India could perhaps be described as 'internal exiles' in Britain where we might appear to be 'at home' but somehow never could be entirely; nor could we be entirely 'at home' in India.

One day last year in Edinburgh I was asked the way by two women at the bus stop. I was going the same way so chatted to them on the bus. When they heard I had lived in Edinburgh for over sixty years, they remarked on my not having a Scottish accent. 'I was born in India,' I explained, 'before Independence'. 'So were we,' they both exclaimed! We chatted a bit more and five minutes later embraced each other as we parted, feeling kindred souls. We didn't need to analyse what it was that we all understood about our lives, which we had in common.

Saying good-bye for ever to servants, friends and companions, who were central to our lives, is a hollowing experience in the heart, whatever age we may be. Yet in some sense such friends never die, because we always remember them as they were and as we were.

Ruth said, 'Whither thou goest I shall go, and where thou lodgest I shall lodge'

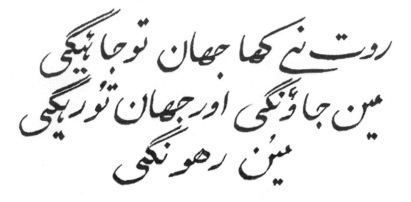

This much-quoted expression of devotion is from the Book of Ruth in the Old Testament. Ruth, who was from the land of Moab, spoke these words to her mother-in-law, Naomi, after they were both left as widows, and Naomi decided to return from Moab to Judah, to Bethlehem, her own home. Ruth went with Naomi and was then remarried to Boaz. Their son was Obed, the father of Jesse, the father of David, who became a great king.

My poem alludes to my having followed my husband into 'the mission field' to live and work alongside him there for an initial five-year tour.

I had been born in India
The man I loved in Scotland
would be a missionary
I had my doubts
about my religious doubts
not about the adventure of Pakistan

On reaching the mission field
I felt myself come home
but daily had to prove
my credentials as one who had
chosen the life for love of a man
rather than love of God

I'm very pleased to meet you
It's a long time since we've seen you
(you've become an Eid Moon)
Will you drink tea on the verandah?

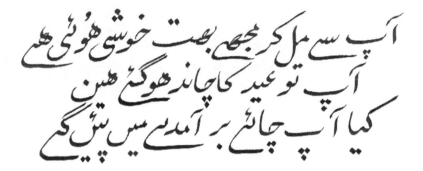

Tea was important in my life and was not always available in the local bazaar, strange as it may seem. I used to save the breakfast tea in a thermos for later in the day. Friends calling was a treat and always unexpected as we had no telephones to make such arrangements.

The Eid new moon signals the end of the month of Ramadan, the month of fasting, and is therefore eagerly anticipated. Someone who has 'become an Eid moon' is therefore long awaited.

Hot dusty weary
the house the road the work
but in the evening
the garden gently cooling
a longed-for friend
and the hornbill watching from the sheesham trees
all I ask is tea on the verandah

This is well water
This is rain water
Boil sufficient water for us to have tea and for me
to wash my hair

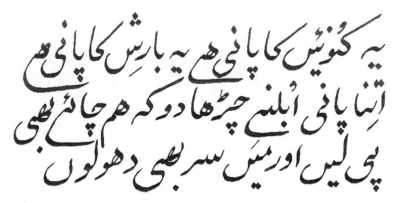

We were lucky to have running cold water in our bungalow. It came from a nearby Persian wheel or well, where a buffalo or ox trod round in a circle while shafted to the buckets going up and down. On our flat roof, where I used to hang out the washing, we could see the Pir Panjal Himalayan ranges in the distance on a clear day in winter. Water from the well was best for drinking, though it had first to be boiled and cooled, whereas water from the rain tank was suitable for washing.

Water drawn from the Persian wheel
the buffalo toiling round and round
tastes of dark – the land – the soil
the sweat – the goodness of the ground

Water collected from roof or garden
from downpour-the clouds crack open in storm
tells of far-off snow ranges
sky – trees – redemption

I was about to come yesterday
but guests arrived so I couldn't

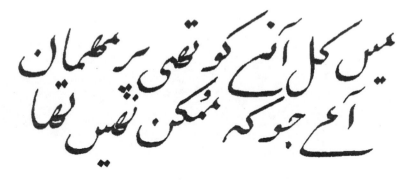

This alludes to the burden of hospitality in the Pakistani tradition and to a proverb about the blanket being too short for the bed, a version of 'cut your coat according to your cloth.' The cost of having visitors, usually relatives who outstayed their welcome, could be ruinous to a family.

Guests expected, excitement
company, gossip, laughter
forget the loneliness
forget the work
so much to tell to ask to share
so much to do
to provide for their every imagined need

Our guests are staying
on days on weeks
our blanket becomes too short for our bed
honour forbids we mention it
the guest is king of the castle

Please don't mention this to anyone

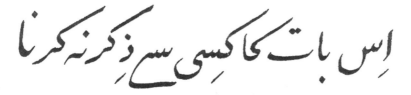

This poem recalls the time when I was alone for three months with my eighteen-month old baby in a little tin-roofed, two-roomed bothy in the foothills of the Himalayas in Murree, 20 miles and 7,000 feet up the mountains from Rawalpindi. This had meant a full day's drive from where we lived in Sialkot and renting the mission car, packing everything we needed, including stove, bedding and crockery, etc. There were half a dozen such houses on the hillside compound, which missionary wives and children rented for the height of the hot season. A watchman was responsible for our safety at night and would sit outside one or other of the houses. I was six months pregnant with a second baby. An old mission servant was with me but didn't live in the house. When the little one was ill, as she was constantly with coughs and fevers, since it was often damp and stormy and life was more or less like camping, I used to feel anxious and lonely. There was no telephone and to go to the clinic was a long walk. On one occasion I was in tears and the old man told me that another Scottish missionary wife, for whom he had worked, had a baby much more seriously ill than mine was and hadn't cried. In fact her baby had died, so that didn't exactly cheer me up! I have set the scene however in the Punjab plains where we lived most of the year and where the *mali*, or gardener, used to come in with flowers from the rather wild garden which surrounded the bungalow. There was no front door and he would just appear, bare-foot, from the verandah, smiling, give me the flowers and disappear again.

But
heat, dust
aching legs
throbbing head
children sick
no privacy
no light, no water
mosquitoes, flies
ants, weevils
the stove smokes
feel like weeping
no phone no friend

The servant sees me:
'the other memsahib never cried
when things were much worse'
then I cry and cry the more
'please don't mention this to anyone'
he won't
his pride and sense of honour
restores my own, a little

The *mali* appears barefoot
silently with sweet peas

Does the watchman stay awake all night?
As far as I know he does

کیا چوکیدار رات بھر جاگتا رہتا ہے؟
جہاں تک مجھے پتہ ہے وہ جاگتا ہے

This poem alludes to an incident which took place when we were leaving the hill station after four months there and a new baby born, only two weeks old. We had a day-long journey ahead of us back to the plains. We packed the mission car as we had done for the journey up, a tight fit, and started off toward the gate of the compound, when we saw the watchman, the *chowkidar*, running and shouting and waving his arms wildly.

He may keep awake all night but he
certainly keeps me awake all night
coughing on the verandah and smoking
hash through a hookah –
Would he be able to save me
from whatever it is that threatens?
Yes
Remember how he came running
wildly waving his arms and shouting?
I had left the sleeping baby behind
when we drove off in the mission car

If it is permitted may I say something?
Take all your stuff and leave

اگر اِجازت ہو تو میں کچھ بولوں ؟

تم سارے سامان سمیت یہاں سے چلے جاؤ

This poem reflects the lack of electricity and the dangers of being exploited ourselves when we were living very simply and when things were often hard or impossible to replace. It incorporates another model sentence which is a quotation referring to John the Baptist in the Gospel of John 5:35.

Take your bedding roll and go
with all that you have taken of ours
under cover of wanting to know about Jesus –
watches, money, coffee, my hurricane lamp

It's the lamp I miss the most

For me *'it was a burning and shining light'*
in dark of night when the child was fevered

Please bring two, two-anna stamped envelopes
from the bazaar
I have to post these letters
What time does the post go?

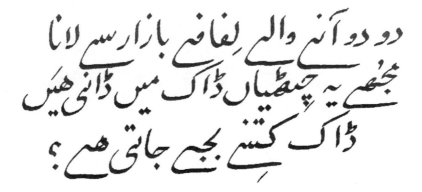

The only contact I had with my parents and other family and friends was by airmail letter, usually a blue airmail letter-form, already stamped. As we had no telephones we needed to write letters locally, too, every day. I wrote every week to my parents, as they did to me. They kept all my letters. Theirs to me were lost when our luggage was burnt on a ship in Liverpool docks in 1968. I was especially homesick when my babies were born and my parents couldn't see them. There was no Post Office at the corner of the road but three miles away on a rough track. I did cycle myself, but couldn't just up and go when I had children to look after. So for buying stamps and posting letters I would look out for someone who was due to be cycling into the city for other reasons. The only other mode of transport was the pony trap or *tonga*.

What time does the post go? I need stamped envelopes
Whom shall I send to the bazaar on a bicycle?
Letters written 'home' week by week and the answer
waited for week after week but we keep each other
alive as ourselves with this flow of words
written in tears in tiredness
in happiness and longing:
'I wish with all my heart
you could see my adorable baby'

These locks have no keys

اِن تالوں کی چابیاں نہیں

I was responsible for the distribution of relief foodstuff from the welfare centre. Sacks of wheat, tins of dried milk, tins of honey and oil came from Church World Service. It had to be stored in the *godown*, or lock-up, then distributed and accounted for. The women, holding their babies, would queue up and give their thumb print by way of receipt. For the wheat, they were given a measure of a bowl filled to the brim and levelled off exactly. It would be poured into their outspread *dopatta* or headscarf. However I also organised for a porridge – made of ground wheat, dried milk, oil and honey – to be cooked on the premises and fed each day to every child under school-age. This was a way of making sure the nourishment reached the children. There were often disputes between the women, as one family would manage to get a double ration if I didn't know that two separate claimants were from one family. Of the hundred or so women who attended the welfare centre I did know each one and visited them in their homes in the surrounding area.

(Quoted from my unpublished autobiography)

Rusty, broken, these locks have forgotten
what they protect: the relief stores.
Some youths have broken into the *godown*
and ransacked the wheatsacks
wheat I must distribute
with exact fairness to each of the women
who come with their babies to the welfare centre
their purple thumb print, their *dopatta* outspread
the bowl brimming, not a grain wasted.

You ought not to have asked me this
You oughtn't to say such things

چاہئے تھا کہ آپ مجھ سے یہ بات نہ پوچھتے
آپ کو ایسی باتیں کرنی نہیں چاہیئں

It wasn't done to question the way that things were done during your first tour of duty, five years, because you couldn't possibly understand the complexities of local life and relationships. This was good advice. I once invited two couples for a meal, who had grown-up children and were friendly and helpful to me. It turned out afterwards that they hadn't been on speaking terms for years, since the son of one had jilted the daughter of the other in an attempted arranged marriage. However the outcome was good. They began to speak to each other again and each of the affected offspring made other marriages.

Why not? What *ought* dictates?
Must we turn our eyes away
questions suppressed, opinions withheld?
Who is giving these orders?
Truth disobeys them

I carry about in my body the marks of Christ

میں اپنے جسم پر مسیح کے داغ لئے پھرتا ہوں

This sentence is a quotation from St Paul, in Galatians 6:17, referring to the *stigmata* or marks of the crucifixion nails on Jesus's resurrected body. The physical and emotional hardship of daily life for me was not easy. It was comforting to feel that it was sacrificial, but for what exactly?

Yes, wounded and pierced
the nails and the spear

but in me the wounds are
lodged in my heart

while my brain ticks over

They met and have gone away together

وہ مل کر چلے گئے ھیں

Every year there was a camp for students run by the Student Christian Movement. This was held in the hills during June. The students were housed in long rectangular wooden huts, girls and boys separate. I was asked to go as a chaperone for the girls, sleeping in the hut with them and queuing for the toilets and washroom in the morning, when they would take ages with their long hair. At the end of the week, buses were sent to take them home. Horror of horrors, a girl and a boy were missing. They kept the bus waiting for a couple of hours. It was a huge worry in that culture.

(Quoted from my unpublished autobiography)

Together they have gone away
away together they have gone
gone they have together

Have they gone together away?

Together gone, together away
together they have, they are,
so there

He said he would do it the next day

اُس نے کہا کہ میَں کل کر دوَں گا

This happens in every culture of course, with workmen in particular.
You gradually learnt who could be relied on and who could not.

and I believed him.
Perhaps he believes in being rather than doing
but you can't do that the next day

He comforted the dying

اُس نے مرتوں کو تسلّی دی

The dying were all around us, particularly children, but also young adults, dying of TB, malaria and other fevers. Girls died in childbirth. Fellow missionaries also died, and my husband and other friends were frequently ill with hepatitis, paratyphoid, mysterious fevers, malaria and dysentery. We were vaccinated frequently, especially for cholera. And there was cancer awaiting the old. But apart from disease, a wonderful missionary doctor was killed in a car crash when the dust at the margins of the single track road blinded the windscreen. Death was ever-present.

Did he reassure them they had not live in vain?
What is a life that is not lived in vain?
'*Vanity of vanities*, saith the preacher'.
Death though, death is not in vain.
It gives abandonment, forgetting
forgiving, forgoing
going before,
that is comfort.

I was glad to cross the ocean and reach Pakistan

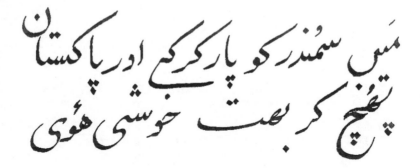

This poem describes the beauty of the environment in the Punjab contrasted with the poverty and sickness of the people.

To hear psalms sung in Urdu to Punjabi tunes and the beat of the
    tabla
the honk honk of the machine which grinds the wheat

To watch sugar cane pulped and boiled in a huge iron cauldron
on a kiln built out in the field
camels feeding under the trees near the village
buffalos washed in the yard which surrounds each cleanly-swept
    house

To see people with pitchers or loads on their heads, walking or
    cycling
palm and mango trees
clear starlit nights
but why does 'god' allow the continual poverty and struggle?
I can't endure the babies dying and still they go on being born
how brave are the women, how kind, and they laugh
they have gathered flowers from a walk in the cool dawn

His coming and going here is not without reason

Found Poem

اُس کا کہاں آنا جانا بے وجہ نہیں

The following is a composition from more of the model sentences. It became a problem whenever the milkman put water in the milk to dilute it. There was a fear of the water being contaminated, even though we boiled the milk before using. Other sentences reflect the continual worry over sick children and poverty, lack of communication causing uncertainty, the need to be self-sufficient and the lovely proverb of the snake and the rope. 'His coming and going not being without reason' might be thought of as referring to our own coming to Pakistan and our going.

May I help you?

Whom shall we send? Which way am I to go?
It's no use going any further. Where shall I put the bedding roll?
Where have you come from? Where do you live?

He may be sick but he comes to work

A person bitten by a snake is afraid of a rope
Perfect love casteth out fear

When a child gets a cough, rub him with a mixture of kerosene and
  mustard seed oil
Give him just fruit juice and milk several times a day

The milkman very dishonestly put water in the milk

We intend to go to Lahore tomorrow
Wait a minute: I'm not ready yet
It's not fitting to spend so much money on a wedding

We had to take our child to the doctor yesterday
He promised he would see us the next day
When there is so much sickness what else can one do?

He has a lot of boys and girls and they have nothing to eat
Please come to see us as soon as possible
Don't you wish to help him?
Yes, but he didn't ask me for help

He bought all the horses
What is the *tonga* hire for an hour?

This girl made her own clothes
It takes seven yards of cloth to make *shalwar-chemise*

He lost two fingers in the fight
That's much too expensive

The Landlord is a good-natured man, but do not insult him
It was my fault. The door came open itself

You may go now. Come again tomorrow
Perhaps they will return by evening
His coming and going here is not without reason

TESSA RANSFORD

With Gratitude to India

I was a baby in India
born among dark eyes and thin limbs
handled by slim fingers
bounced by bangles
and held high among the turbans,
surrounded by the light sari
black knot of hair
suggestion of spice,
wrapped up only by those songs
that spiral the spirit out of the dust
and lay it down again to sleep.

I crawled among bright toenails
ticked off ants by the gross
or touched the lizard in his cold quickness;
toddled past wilting bougainvillaea
to watch hoopoes on the mai-dan,
caught flashes of minivet, oriole and bulbul
and peered up into huge flowers
on tree after tree
as I broke into their shade.

Never left with a strange
babysitter
I was part of the parties, parades,
the bazaar,
could swallow the stenches and listen
to the poetry of bargaining;
hearts' desire was to drink cool water
or chew a sugar-cane
and flap off the flies.

I had dysentery, sickness, paleness
boiled buffalo milk,
no welfare vitamins, no plastic pants.
The sun was a fiend, the rain was a friend
the stars only just out of reach.

Expressions were always changing:
a smile latent in sorrow
and a love in anger;
tears happened with laughter
but patience presided over every mood.

To have first found the world
in abundant India
is my life's greatest privilege.

I have always been grateful for starting my life in a country where children are welcome and accepted, and babies are sung to, carried and patted to sleep. Three of my own children, born in Pakistan, also had this privilege. The poem draws on memories of my own and my experience as a mother. In Scotland we tended to be expected to apologise for children and not let them disturb adult life, though this is indeed changing as men begin to take more part in their children's upbringing.

The Dhobi's Dog

Dhobi ka kutta na ghar ka na ghat ka
(The washerman's dog belongs neither to house nor riverside)

The dhobi's dog will return from riverbank in the sun
to the house, but not lie down; to and fro he'll trot
panting, semi-wild, hither and thither recalled,
never petted, fondled, either hot or cold.
Does he belong? To whom? Dhobi-ji sends him home,
Bibi-ji won't give him room. Such is my lot.

Born and reared in India, comforted by ayah
on some cool verandah of lofty bungalow
with charpai and degchi, decanter and serahi,
enervated, dusty, the whining mosquito,
black ants and red, huge fans overhead:
when all was done and said, the British had to go.

In Scotland I froze: hands, feet, nose,
in thick uneasy clothes at dour boarding school:
a wind-resistant, dismal, stern, redoubtable,
grey-stone-wall life exemplified by rule;
embarrassed to embrace, weep, laugh, kiss:
was I of this race? from such a gene pool?

I lived in Pakistan, land of the Mussulman,
governed by the Koran. I learnt Punjabi,
dressed in shalwar, travelled to Lahore,
joined in zabur, lived on dal-chapati:
but didn't my passport say 'British, born Bombay'
however long my stay in Sialkot or Karachi?

I like the way I speak, the voice my thoughts make,
yet Scottish folk are quick to think me English.
I've lived here (sixty) years (Anderson forebears
and Glasgow Macalisters – that's buksheesh!)
Still my language finds no place, no ethnic dress or face:
I plead my special case and thus I finish.

The Dhobi's dog belongs nowhere

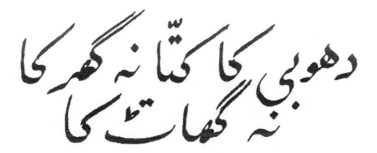

دھوبی کا کتا نہ گھر کا
نہ گھاٹ کا

As is implied by the proverb 'The Dhobi's Dog', it is impossible ever to lose the connection with our early childhood. I consider that my Indian self, in its adjustment to Scotland, had a hard time, but eventually found the solution in poetry although even then I didn't seem to quite fit into any of the established categories of 'Scottish poet'.

My Indian Self

Let me be
myself my
Indian self
that goes to extremes
from garland to ashes
Himalaya to desert
mango to maize

Let me wear the silks
the sandals and the gold.
Let me dip my fingers
in the bowl of desire
even here in the puritan
corners of my dwelling

Let me reclaim
myself; I cannot
be curtailed;
extravagance is my form
not my style;
intensity is how
my pulse is rated

My body is myself
however ageing;
I love the way it has borne
with me all these years
and given nothing less
than life itself to others

Happiness is tropical and
love is a house with wide verandahs.
Joy is my element:
I pass it through the test
of water, fire, air
and bring it back to earth.

When I was fifteen I found, quite by chance, the poems of Rabindranath Tagore in the school library. Of all the thousands of books it was *Gitanjali* which somehow called me to select it. I was overcome by its affect on me and did not mention it to any of my friends, reading it in the library during 'break' rather than taking it out. Later I managed to find other books of Tagore's in second-hand bookshops in Edinburgh. Looking back, I felt that finding Tagore had given expression to an 'Indian self' which had been suppressed since my coming to Britain for the first time in 1944 as a child but especially since going to boarding school in 1948. I had been writing poems since the age of six and while at school, so finding Tagore was almost a recognition of my poetic self too, the *dichten und denken* that helped to reconcile the emotional force-fields of India and Scotland in my life.

(Quoted from my unpublished autobiography)

Set Loose

A company of long grey snakes
slides through child-high grassland
near Bangalore. The grasses roll
like waves but when the snakes
have passed they stand undamaged.

Children slept veiled in mosquito-nets
and on the ceiling a fan slow-whirled.
A cobra was coiled where I stood
to open the skylight, untwisting
a thin cord to let in the Indian night.
It had entered by the water-sluice
where bathtubs were emptied. Why did men
rise up from their string beds to kill it
then and there and cover it where it lay?

They came early to bury it next morning
in case a dog should eat it and fall dead
(as if they cared about the life of dogs).
It was a ritual: snakes must be killed
even while they sleep, innocently coiled.

Now I am disentangling the ropes
that open the sky, while men
and children sleep. Now I take up
the coiled serpent with its crushed head
and set it loose to ripple through the fields.

It doesn't matter

كوئی بات نہیں

There was a snake in our bedroom, a yard long, when we returned at midnight from a trip to Lahore and back from Sialkot. I saw it as I was untwisting the cord which opened the high skylight. My husband killed it with our daughter's toy hockey-stick. It was covered with a tin bowl and left there to be buried in the morning.

(Quoted from my unpublished autobiography)

This experience left a deep impression on me and resulted in the poem many years later. The poem also draws on another image from early childhood of a group of snakes moving swiftly through long grass.

A Kind of Reincarnation

In Scotland all these years
I knew my Indian Self
but as a myth almost, a shadow, a shrunken self
from which I drew nonetheless
the golden thread of poetry.

In Delhi now I find it is growing,
taking me over, a metamorphosis:
what shall I turn into?
Perhaps a piece of material
handwoven to hide the knotting
or a basket chair or a samovar serving
Kashmir tea with almonds?
Or shall I become the dusty leaf of a
roadside tree waiting for water and fire?

I realise my Indian Self will be faded
and insignificant and yet
will gradually nudge
my Scottish Self into shade.

The language flows through me today as if
a tap were turned on in my body.
I find myself saying words for
because, why, however, whenever,
how many, where and what as well as
I'm not feeling well
I'm very tired
It doesn't matter
Well done and thank you for your trouble
The electricity isn't working
In an hour or two I'll be ready
Which path leads to the gate?

Then I walk over a raj-built bridge
with eight arches and slowly,
sensing each step in my sandals
and Indian-made tartan skirt,
I gently pass through the gate.

When in Delhi, for its International Literary Festival in December 2008, I found by the third day that the Urdu I had spoken fluently forty years before was taking over in my head.

It was a curious experience, making me feel I had no control over it. Although the language is called Hindi in Delhi, it is essentially the same language as Urdu, and although Delhi is in India it is part of the Punjab, as was the area of Pakistan where I had lived during the early 1960s. The surroundings and the language therefore were familiar. Delhi is also full of mementos of the British Raj, under which my parents had lived and worked in India for twenty-five years and I had spent my early childhood. Therefore in Delhi I felt I was transported into both my own past and that of my parents simultaneously, while also operating in the present at the literary festival. I consider that my becoming a poet is probably linked to the experiences of the emotional cultures of India and Scotland, which I had somehow to unite within me in a creative way.

Sea-Scenes from my life

What did I see? A dog being drowned
black and dangly down by the harbour in Bombay.
I was coming on six and looked out of the window.

Not long after, a cargo ship in the docks exploded.
It had been carrying dynamite packed below bales of cotton.
Everyone thought the Japs had attacked (1944).
All the rescuers rushed to the harbour
when a second explosion killed them.
Bodies were blown all over the city.

The floor-to-ceiling doors of the room I was in
fell crashing down;
servants came running, my mother came running,
I was unhurt.
My father hurried back from work expecting to find
his family dead. We were safe:
the doors and windows blown out and
gold bars scattered over the city.
They were laying out the dead in the hospital corridors.

The day was announced we had waited for and we steamed away
in convoy heading for Britain, an unknown country to me.
We wept goodbye to our servants in tears, to our little dachshunds,
our ancient cat. Packed in cabins for women and children
we contracted diseases; weak and fearful lest the torpedoes
attacked. At Port Said I watched from the rails as Italian prisoners
dressed in grey, were marshalled into the hold.
I swung from the bunks and cut my lip; then fevered
with tonsilitis endured the rest of the long long trip.

One day when I was five, coming on six, I was playing by myself in a big upstairs room in the Mint House, Bombay, when suddenly there was a shaking and the huge ceiling-high door cracked down the middle and came off its hinges, while rushing wind came in through broken windows. Most rooms of Mint House were high-ceilinged to be cool, with huge double doors which could be opened to allow every breath of air possible. This may have been a playroom, or a bedroom, because its window looked over the Alexandra Dock, just over a mile away, and a little bit of shore and sea, where I once, to my horror, saw a man drowning a dog.

When the doors cracked and the windows broke I stood there in surprise until my mother and some of the servants came running, relieved that I was alright. Nobody knew what had happened. Then my father came running back from the Mint, whence the windows had blown out and machinery had been thrown about. Having seen the ball of flame and smoke, he expected to find his house in devastation and his family hurt or killed. We all gathered under the stairs, the family, the servants and their families, a German-Jewish refugee staying with us and another woman convalescing. Screaming terrified people were rushing up the road. Our friends thought we would be dead. Thousands of people were killed or injured or lost their homes, businesses and belongings that day. Since a Japanese attack on India was feared at the time, many people suspected that this was happening and fled the city.

The 'Bombay Explosion' occurred on 14 April 1944 in the Victoria Dock in Bombay harbour, when SS *Stikine* caught fire and was destroyed in two giant blasts, scattering lethal debris and sinking eleven other ships.

(Details from www.holysmoke.org/great-bombay.htm Lawrence Wilson, 1979).

The 'Bombay Explosion' delayed our sailing which had been scheduled for 15th April. When we did sail, toward the end of April, it was on the HMS *Otranto* in convoy, taking five weeks to arrive at Liverpool just before D-day, 6th June. My mother referred to it as 'the ghastly voyage home'.

(Quoted from my unpublished autobiography)

Homeless or Homeful

Before I was ten I lived in eleven dwellings
and eleven more before I was thirty and three.
Twenty-two homes to live in and leave
in thirty years, and you ask me where I come from!

I hear of homeless immigrants and know that I know.

We rented lonely dark places, stayed with relations,
were 'paying guests' with friends or strangers
and this was in war-years, the rationing,
the making-do and managing,
waiting still and hoping times,
not quite sure and maybe if and
thankful for small mercies times
when 'home' was where we were just now,
where my mother was and where she made
what beauty that she could as best she could
and never thought it not *worthwhile*.

A garden or a picture, books, colour,
the book of nature too and always
getting rid of clutter, all we couldn't carry
and a clearing-out and placing-in of us:
our stories, self-respect, the friends
we had to leave, the memories that nobody
could share with us, our dreams, dream-houses
and our need to hold together to exist.

I've said goodbye to homes where I have worked
to make them clean and habitable.
Perhaps I was a slave to them, never ceasing
in the daily task of damming dereliction.
There is some freedom in forsaking them,
in letting run unravelled the woven toil
of years, made up of minutes, that was
tight, so coiled around me.

I alone now know about those places
which I laboured to sustain and then destroyed
by simply ceasing, moving on. What marks
of me remain will be anonymous.

Don't ask us where we come from; where we go
is more important. Yet we leave a trail,
a string of beauty, broken, that we made,
homeless yet homeful, scattered now.

My father returned to India, after six months' leave, in September
1944 and my darling brother, aged only eight, fresh from India,
was sent to boarding school. My mother rented half a farmhouse
in Childswickham, near Broadway, Worcestershire. It was dark,
damp, cold, stone-floored, had no electricity and it was winter. I
was sent to the local village school, where I very quickly learned to
read, from Barbara with whom I shared a bench. I enjoyed the
buzz of the village school, which involved playground rough and

tumble such as being chased by the boys. My mother and I lived in one room to keep warm, where she tried to learn to cook after her years in India. I was my mother's companion and treated as such by her. The war was still on and planes flew over. One day, as we were walking home on a footpath, a sudden roar and an aeroplane came crashing down one field away. It went up in flames. My mother said 'stay here' and immediately ran towards it, as did one or two others who had seen it. In my vision she was running towards the flames and I would never see her again. I began screaming and crying. Someone passing by or watching comforted me and eventually she came back and blamed herself for having left me like that, obeying her instinct to go to try to help. It was a British plane which had crashed and no-one was alive. I can still see the crashed plane, the flames and my mother's back-view running towards them.

After that winter at Childswickham we moved. My mother had found a girls' school, St Christophers, in Burnham-on-Sea, Somerset, which she was advised would be more suitable for me. We stayed in a hotel to begin with. I remember going to school the first day, when there was a party for the war in Europe having ended, and cowering in terror and shyness in a corner of a huge gym hall. In the hotel my mother and I shared a room and meagre rations. My mother didn't take milk in her tea, but saved any milk which was put on a tray to give to me. When this was discovered they stopped putting milk on her tea-tray. We then found rooms looking over the sea with Mrs Feaver and her daughter Mary. I wrote one of my first poems there, watching the path made by the moon on the water.

We then moved into a boarding house in Berrow, along the coast from Burnham... We couldn't stay there for various reasons, one of which was that we impulsively bought a Dachshund puppy! We were taken in by Mr and Mrs Day in the house next door. They provided us with one room, where I shared a double bed with my mother.

(Quoted from my unpublished autobiography)

Questionnaired

'Tell me again – the name of your wife,
her age both now and when you were married,
children – alive, dead or miscarried,
the name of her father and your mother,
everyone's sister and anyone's brother;

what did you say was the name of your wife?
Is she the second or was she the first?
Did she speak what had been rehearsed?

Income tax – how many dependents?
We'll have to make a few amendments
to previous statements now denied.
Did you declare what you couldn't hide?

By the way, what's the name of your wife?

Is this your present or previous life?'

'Sir, I have told you, I tell you once more:
I still have the one wife I had before.
It's not a question of reincarnation,
simply a matter of immigration.

Dream or nightmare, this is my life
as I mouth
            the sounds
                of the name
                    of my wife.'

This poem was written in the 1970s when I was asked occasionally to act as an interpreter for Pakistanis in Scotland, mainly women in hospital, but on this occasion for the immigration service. I was appalled by the ignorance of the questioners about the culture of Pakistan. The man being questioned was applying to bring his nephews over as a priority over his wife and daughters. This poem has been anthologised a few times and also translated into Danish.

Indian Women at Windermere

Indian women at Windermere
why carry plastic buckets and pans
stooped and bending low
when you know
how to sail along like swans
your loads aloft as head-gear?

Oldish women in walking shoes,
saris, coats and spectacles,
with wealthy westernised sons
Indians
living in modern bungalows –
how much of yourselves have you had to lose?

If I were you I would wish to be
inconspicuous yet walking tall;
no slavery
to nationality
whether in Britain or Bengal –
head high and both hands free.

I saw these Indian women at a campsite near Windermere and thought of how in India they would carry burdens elegantly on their heads having their hands free for their children. I didn't like to see them becoming in this way bowed down by 'westernisation'.

Indian music concert in Edinburgh church, 2007

Lalgudi Gjr. Krishanan
Lalgudi Vijayalakshmi
Somasundara Desigar

South Indian ragas played on violins
With mridangam, oval drum
O quench our thirst

Brother and sister sit for two hours
cross-legged, barefooted
flexible wrists and flying fingers
O melt our bones

Virtuoso improvisation
exchange of gifts in rhythm and sound
applause accepted with humility
O hear our prayer

'The lesson endeth' for tonight
on our upright chairs in this reason-
worshipping, Scottish church
O restore our sense

I attended this concert in St Andrew's and St George's Church in George Street, Edinburgh. It felt as if some aspects of my life had come full circle when Indian musicians, sitting cross-legged at eye level, could entrance an audience of mainly Edinburgh Indians in a Scottish Presbyterian church originally built for the proclamation of 'the Word' from a high pulpit. As late as the nineteenth century some churches in Edinburgh did not even allow hymns to be sung. It felt as if 'sense' was being restored.

Childbirth

Jesus born in a stable. Sakina's baby
too, born for seclusion in the cattle
section of her clean-swept dung-washed home
built of sun-baked mud bricks beside
the well beneath the peepul tree; or
in Lewis in her blackhouse Mairi's son
born amid the peat-smoke safe and warm
born into a family, a creature among creatures.

What child can save us now on
our deteriorating planet from wretched
battles over oil and water? What star
will now outshine our religiosity?
What re-mind-set for the moneyed globe
to invest in love and save our planet?
foreboding, forgoing and forbearance.

When we visit a woman who has had a baby, the mother is in the darkest corner of the house, possibly in the part used by the buffalo, and the house is anyway dark. The baby will be invisible under a heavy quilt made of stuffed cotton which the woman has on her bed. The baby sleeps with the mother until the next one is born. The woman will not go out for six weeks.

(Quoted from my unpublished autobiography)

In a Scottish thatched Black House or a Pakistani mud house there are often two sections, one being for shelter for the cattle. At time of childbirth the cattle are put out and the birth will take place in that section to give privacy.

The Water-Carriers

A water-carrier, meeting another, asked him for some of his water.
The latter said, 'Why don't you drink your own?' The first said,
'Give me some of your water, for I am sick of my own.'
from *The Conference of the Birds* (Farid ud-Din Attar)

A drop, a pearl
from your cup poured
better than fountain
rain or cloud;

as my soul,
disquieted,
seeks to drink,
so pure it flows
through all, to sink
or rise again,
but never rests,
save in the valley
of emptiness.

Heavy the weight
our own life fills.
I offer my cup –
it brims and spills
your thirst to slake:

we give, we take.

The water-carriers story appears in *The Conference of the Birds*, a Sufi classic from the twelfth century and shows how, as humans, we give each other energy only through interaction and inter-dependence. It is even as Gerard Manley Hopkins wrote, 'selfyeast of spirit a dull dough sours'.

In Pakistan we sometimes lived in accommodation where there was no running water. In the hostel for the missionary language school in Murree in the foothills of the Himalayas, a water-carrier would climb a ladder outside our room with a huge cow- or ox-skin full of water slung across his back and empty it into a tank. We had to make this last, whether for washing ourselves or our clothes, until his next visit, which might be a few days. The heavily-laden water-carriers, or *bishtis*, would be bent nearly double as they laboured up and down the mountainside town.

Kashmir

You speak with me in dream – eastern ascetic man
commune with me whatever we seem to say
    when I ask you where you come from
        turning you look at me telling 'Kashmir'.

High land of sapphires, walnut and mulberry
whose lakes reflect the hills in their violet depths
    glaciers melt to crystal rivers
        kingfishers skim amid water lilies.

The Fisher King may dwell in the Shalimar
and we catch fire – to selve and to bear the light
    whose the face we each reflect?
        Jesus the one and the thousand thousand.

Kashmir afar I love and remember you
fine wool, fine rice, fine silk such as dreamers find
    once in life and ever long for –
        now I must rest in the bluebird's promise.

Kashmir is noted for an abundance of kingfishers. We had a holiday there in 1967, staying first on a houseboat on Lake Dal and then camping at Pahalgam in the mountains. Gerard Manley Hopkins's poem 'As Kingfishers Catch Fire' (used as the title of a novel by Rumer Godden set in Kashmir) uses the verb 'selves' and suggest that Jesus is present in 'ten thousand places'. There is also a tradition that Jesus may have visited Kashmir. The poem is written in the Alcaic metre.

Why allow salt water to rust your heart?

written at the time of the invasion of Afghanistan in 2001

RUMI, whom I revere
enter, entrance me now
or nine hundred years ago

Scholar, poet, mystic
the searing of love's flame
your dervish dance, your extreme

Finding and losing in Shams
god-in-a-person, abyss
absence and nothingness

Unbegun and unended
the soul river will flow
as laughter, as sorrow

You are a child refugee
fleeing Afghanistan
the terror of Genghis Khan

Slave of glory your name
Jalaluddin, of no country
but love and fanatic poetry

Are these words or tears?
Why allow my heart to rust?
Drench me out of the dust

The title is a quotation from a poem of Rumi's. Mowlana Jalaluddin Mohammed (known as Rumi) was born in Balkh in 1207 in what is now Afghanistan. After his family spent five years as refugees fleeing from the Mongols they settled in Konya in the province of Rum in what is now Turkey. Rumi became a respected Sufi scholar and religious leader until, at the age of 37, upon meeting the dervish Shams of Tabriz, he turned to poetry amid the intoxication of love-longing for the mystic presence of the Beloved.

The Persian Carpet

The real gardens are in the heart
Jalaludin Rumi

Dawn begins with a hymn, birds and clouds, music and flowers
and the crested cockerel of day crows us to prayer

Flowers are lavish jewels in the meadow to glint in sunbeams and
     dance
transfigured in chalice inlaid with topaz and pearl

Deep-eyed deer and squirrels, from serpent to valiant steed
sanctuary for lives in abundant measure

Rocks stand piled on rocks, top crazy, the many mansions of
     heaven
pavilions for shade and raiment of green and gold

Medallions of lapis lazuli are hidden aquifers
where rivers run of honey, milk, forgiveness

Dark shadowy cypresses, willows weep and grieve
pear blossom and *parvaneh* adorn the parkland

Water channels keep flowing however arid and barren the wind
mapped on the carpets, they irrigate the gardens

Sevenfold walls of mud or stone protect from the King of Locusts
who wears disguises in every cared-for plot

The first wall is our family – the second our teachers –
the third our friends – the fourth our home-felt place –
the fifth is our hope – the sixth is our kindness –
the seventh is a lighted lamp in the tent of the blessed
at the feet of the knower and lover of ancient wisdom

Roses may wither but poems endure – buildings decay and fall
yet the word is hidden encoded over the earth
In devotion we walk the line the square the dome the turret the
    fountain
to kneel and adore our carpet, our paradise garden

At a conference on Persian carpets at the Burrell Gallery in Glasgow in March 2010, I learnt how the carpets are designed to represent a Persian garden, which is also the image for Paradise. The gardens were built above aquifers in the desert and had seven walls around them to protect from sandstorms and other destructive forces. They were precious indeed. Within the gardens there is abundant life of every kind, fed by irrigation channels and shaded by trees. As you kneel to pray on your carpet or rug you are therefore sacramentally entering paradise.

The King of the Locusts is a term for the forces of death or destruction, Apollyon or Satan himself. Thus the fertility and life-giving resources of nature, dependent on water, are at the heart of all religion. I added my own interpretation of the seven walls, making it a personal poem for myself. I have artist and translator Jila Peacock to thank for inviting me to the conference, which was uplifting and enlightening.

Butterfly

پروانه

Islam

min
a
ret
place
of
fire
pharos
beacon
light
beckoning
the faithful
five times
a day
on and off
flashing
and
filtered
through carved
mashrabeya
of the night

purifies
mind's light
of reason
lifts
pointed
slender
stem
of feeling

cleaves
the sky
spiralling
like smoke

above the domed
house of gathered
living

above the court
yard
of cleansed hearts
above pillared
terraces of prayer

where forehead
stoops to dent
hallowed dust
and palms open
holding nothing back

through minaret
like lightning
conducted

flames
one
true thought
ALLAH

The minaret is architecturally inspired by the lighthouse, particularly the *pharos* of ancient Egypt. When visiting a friend in Egypt I explored some of the lovely mosques of Cairo, where light and shade are as integral to the aesthetic whole as the arches and court-yards. In the poem I think of the Call to Prayer from the minaret five times a day as being comparable to the flashing on and off of the beam from a lighthouse.

The Shanty-Town Kids of Karachi

The Shanty-town kids of Karachi
that great port
had never been down to the beach
a good hour's drive from the city
where the rich
owned weekend chalets and where
giant turtles crawled up the sands
at hightide midnight in Spring
to lay their hoard-hole of eggs.

The children lived in a dusty encampment
with one water pump in heat and disease;
their parents swept the marble floors of the rich
or the airport halls
and children minded the babies while their parents
minded the babies of others.

In rags and shoeless, the shanty-town kids
eighty or more
went down to the sea one day in a hired bus.
Sheltered in a beach hut by special arrangement
we took them down to the water;
they waded in with their clothes on
soon dried again in the heat;
they frolicked and played and laughed and cried
then fed and tended we drove them back
to their hovels.

I was planning a beach picnic for the Pakistani children of 6–12 years old in the shanty town at Drigh Road near Karachi airport, hiring the convent bus for 80 rupees from 9am to 5pm and taking all the food, water, clothes and amusements required. Kay Hussein, the mother of my daughter Meg's friend Amby, was trying to run a chicken farm and gave me free eggs for the picnic. The Pakistani *padri* and his family came, as well as Meg's teacher and her children and the wife of the Immigration officer. It was a hard day's work for us but we had the use of a beach hut, and it was wonderful to see all the children running down to the water, some just going into the waves in their clothes which soon dried out. It was an hour's hot drive down to the beach from the city centre and the shanty town children had never seen the sea, never been to the beach.

(Quoted from my unpublished autobiography)

Blessings on the big day

نے دِن مُبارک ہو

Christmas and Children in Sialkot, Pakistan as I remember celeb-
rating in the 1960s.

(Sialkot is in the North East of the Punjab, near the Kashmir
border. I worked in a welfare centre for women and children in a
part of the city called Christiantown. Rice was for special occasions,
the staple food being the *chapati*.)

Blessings on the big day

(bare din mumbarak ho)

a bowl of steaming rice
see it cooking in the courtyard
ladled out a Christmas taste
for the children of the compound
never mind the dirt and flies
it makes a feast, a concert

for Christmastime brings cold winds
from Kashmir and storms of rain
but today the sun shines gently
and the goat-stew curried gravy
simmers with potatoes
carrots and tomatos,
let's lick our lips again

halleluya
beat the *tabla*
sweep the house
a bright *dopatta*
coloured clothes
with tinselled border

spangly shoes from the bazaar
fresh milk from the buffalo
shawl washed at the river bank
hair washed at the common pump
fetch the baby, run and follow
sing psalms and clap hands
dogs and donkeys flick their ears
the camel kneels
the vulture wheels
we live for the day today
sweetmeats and jamboree
jerseys given from charity
sit in shade beneath the trees

Santa Claus is nothing here
chimneys, candles, twigs of fir
presents, dancing, parties.
Here it's staving off hunger
hope of cure
for dysentery, malaria
hope that grain-growing weather
give us lentils and chapatis

sugar cane is in the fields
sweet and sticky, juicy yields
irrigation channels flow
chrysanthemums and dahlias
in pots on verandas
poinsettia bushes glow

new life, new sun
divine become human
earth blessed anew
we accept and know
this is somehow true

DON'T MENTION THIS TO ANYONE

I wrote this poem in aid of the Sick Kids Hospital in Edinburgh and read it at their Carol Service in St Cuthbert's Church in December 2009. It was first published in *The Gift of Words* in support of The Sick Kids Friends Foundation. It describes Christmas celebrations in the villages of the Punjab during our time there in the 1960s. My daughters loved the 'spangly shoes', one of them refusing to take them off at bedtime!

Entwined

Guardians of India, idealists yet surgeons
or engineers, my ancestors to six generations
spent lives, sweat, tears, wives and children.
Home was a word in the heart, almost strange.

My medical grandpa: the only surviving child from eleven;
my own three siblings died. How precious I was
to my parents. My mother's passion the birds and trees,
bright flowers that bloomed in the dust *tra la*.

India and Scotland are entwined like a Kashmir shawl
round my life. The knot cannot be unravelled but
can uncoil like a snake, start up like the brain-
fever-bird that disturbs any chance of rest.

My Ransford ancestors served in India as surgeons or engineers and my own grandfather was the only surviving child of eleven to Surgeon-General John Ransford and his wife Emily Davis, who lived in Kanpur or Cawnpore as it was called then. They finally left India in 1859 when my grandfather, Thomas, was nine years old. My mother wrote a series of illustrated books on the birds, flowers and flowering trees of India entitled *Nurseries of Heaven*. The brain-fever-bird (common hawk cuckoo) has a maddening call on rising notes which are repeated over and over.

Two-Way

I think of India and yearn for my childhood,
my parents brave and hardworking who wilted
there, my siblings who died. Here I found
a country reserved as if promised and jilted.

How could I go back now? I made a craft
to sail through the world built from books
of poetry. A flimsy vessel it stays afloat
through storm and piracy, between the rocks.

That's how my ancestor sailed in a paddle steamer
from Clyde to Malay, became Harbour Master.
Practical, kind, principled, tough, yet prey
to ideals, we're set to go on like that: two-way.

Three of my siblings died, before my brother and I were born in Bombay. My parents were alone in India without family. All my grandparents died before I was born while my parents were away from them. It was a life of exile in many aspects. Another ancestor, John Anderson, sailed the Clyde Paddle-Steamer, The Shandon, to Melbourne and then to Singapore in the 1850s. He became harbour-master in Singapore. The grown-up daughter of his first wife – who had died before he left on the Shandon – remained in Greenock and Glasgow and was my great grandmother, Jessie Anderson, who married shipping director, William Boyd Macalister.

Faded Indian Bedspread

My faded Indian bedspread
threadbare and washed out
I would not exchange
for a luxurious quilt

With ancient flowering pattern
and cotton endurance
to another generation
its workaday presence

There is nothing more beautiful than a handwoven Indian bed-spread. They were spread on the string *charpais*, or wooden frame beds, that we all used in the Punjab, and where folk would sit at any time of day. This was like the armchair in a western house-hold, the centre of gossip and daily life.

Going Nowhere

Travelling to Kashmir
the delectable mountains
five days' journey
through the burning plains

At Delhi a telegram
her little girl was ill
she turned back home
turned away from the hills

And I see those who give
up on promised lands
turn back because they have
the present on their hands

My mother was going on a trip to Kashmir and had got as far as Delhi from Bombay, when she received a telegram to say that I was ill, so she returned and never saw Kashmir. When I was able to visit Kashmir in my turn I felt sad that my mother never managed to do so. It is indeed a paradise. As women we always have the present on our hands to deal with and often cannot follow our dreams. But the present perhaps becomes our dream.

Godavari River Valley
Western Ghats, near Nasik, India

after an oil painting on canvas painted by my mother,
Torfrida Ransford, in the 1930s.

This picture has been restored to us
sacred river, sent us *now*
the Godavari river painted by
our mother long ago

Her work, her hand and eye
rippling water in the Indian heat
mindful every stroke from brush or knife
pastel colours chosen, flow of line

Now circulates like water
this captured painted *now*
on canvas, fragile
to materialise and heal

Thank you mother universe
song of the earth
ewig ewig

Nasik was a hill region north of Bombay, the hot bustling city where my parents were based. My mother painted this river scene from a black-and-white photograph, conjuring the delicate pastel shades on hard-board in oils. The painting returned to our family, after being lost, over a decade after she died, with its healing message at a time of need. The Godavari is one of India's sacred rivers, in which to bathe brings healing.

Sweeping

written in Lodi Gardens, Delhi, on 18 December 2008

Everywhere in Delhi someone is sweeping
women and men with long fibre brooms sweep
pavements, walkways, paths and
beneath the trees or over the grass
with long twig besoms;
they clear the water-channels and allow
hoses to seep upon you silently like snakes;
indoors there are boys who continually swish to and fro
with long-handled mops across halls and corridors
along verandas.

Is life a path that must be swept
each day of each day's concerns
as well as afflictions, ill-omens?
At first I thought it obsessive, but now
I see this leisurely brushing as
peaceful, rhythmical, tender, needful.
It prepares the way:
let me not sweep it aside.

The presence of sweepers – and of dust – is overwhelming in Delhi, indeed everywhere in India. Sweepers are also traditionally from the outcaste caste or the lowest caste and are treated as 'untouchable' by the other castes. Yet they make life possible, cleaning up after and preparing the way for others.

In Christian circles, where I lived and worked in Pakistan, we did not have this mentality and most of the Christians with and for whom we worked were descended from Hindu outcastes three generations or more back. Muslims, too, although they have rich and poor, as we do, do not have a caste system in the same way and, indeed, consider all as equal before Allah, and that it is a duty to give alms to the poor.

Lodi Gardens, Delhi

Gardeners sleep in the midday sun
on winter lawns by the bedded plants
watering cans at their side

Fishtail palms let down their fronds
and the bottle-brush tree opens
its creviced bark to ants and insects

A bowl of water for birds is balanced
in the roots of a flame tree

A little white dog is curled like an egg
in a pile of leaves

Hoses snake over mud-packed paths
between glasshouses and
decaying memorial domes

The air, the smell, the grass, the ground
earnest students and young mothers
loving couples and family groups

My solitary presence like a shadow
reclaiming the past, my past,
India's past, yet ever completely
present

It is normal to have a siesta in the middle of the day in tropical countries, where the cool of the day in the early morning is when work is best done. In Lodi Gardens in Delhi, where I spent a day walking and writing, it was touching to see the many gardeners lying on the grass having their siesta in the pleasant sun of December. I felt like a ghost of myself and of the Raj as I walked there alone among the cheerful groups.

Sweet and Sad

Children of India we chattered the lingo
water and dust plants and flowers
as verandah players
insect crawlers bird callers
with kindly people smelling of spice who
would squat at our level or carry us
swaying barefooted and cool

Children of India
we ran in and out with our brown-limbed friends
sat beside them on charpai or durry
yes, the chapatis slapped together
nimbly the rice juice-laden fruits
sugary tea coconut sweets

Born as survivors siblings who died
children of India we never went back
or home or where our lives began
or travelling back we were awkward and old
language slippage friends dispersed
emerging as pictures fuzzy ghostly
held in the mind for generations
in sepia light of all that was passed

Children of India we never returned
but nor did we lose that strange
intermingled scented colourful
wearied drenched dried-out tested
born to die by-gone gone by
tears in smiles good-bye, gone, good-bye

اس کا یہاں آنا جانا بے وجہ نہیں

**Rug of a Thousand Colours
Poems inspired by the
Five Pillars of Islam by
two contemporary Scottish
writers each translating
the other**
Tessa Ransford and Iyad Hayatleh
ISBN 978-1-908373-24-3 PBK £8.99

*Islam is not a religion of rituals and
rites only, but a method for living the
entire life.*
IYAD HAYATLEH

A powerful exploratory poem-
sequence from a Palestinian
poet living in Glasgow and an
established Scottish poet which
creates a vivid tapestry. It explores
their responses to the Five Pillars
of Islam and reflects their cultural
backgrounds and views. We find,
for instance, Hajj and Pilgrimage
combine to form shared
experience, and Chaucer is in
dialogue with the Qur'an for the
first time.

Featuring a series of poems both in
English and Arabic, this collection
is a conversation between two
poets, two languages and two
cultures. As each poet translates
the other, unpredictable but
revealing symmetries begin to
emerge.

Not Just Moonshine
New and Selected Poems

Tessa Ransford
ISBN 978-1-906307-77-6 £12.99 PBK

When I returned from India to Scotland, first as a child and again as an adult after eight years in Pakistan during my twenties, the juxtaposition of these complementary emotional force-fields precipitated in me the writing, or making, of poetry.
TESSA RANSFORD

This book celebrates Tessa's work over the four decades up to 2008. The selection draws attention to the authenticity and emotional integrity in her writing, her lightness of touch and openness to ideas and the world around her. The development of Tessa's style and technique becomes clear through the recurrent themes of her poetry; motherhood, destiny, nature and love.

Either as an introduction to Tessa's poetry or as a culmination of years of reading her work, *Not Just Moonshine* represents a substantial body of work from one of Scotland's most accomplished and engaging poets.

What is striking about her development as a poet is not only the unity of her work – the 'unusual purity of vision' early identified by Alan Bold – but its continuing openness to the influences of the world around her.
A.C. CLARKE

Ragas and Reels
Visual and Poetic Stories of
Migration and Diaspora

Poems by Bashabi Fraser, with photographs by Hermann Rodrigues
ISBN 978 1 908373 34 2 PBK £9.99

The rhythmic imagery of Bashabi Fraser tells the intricate stories hidden in the portraits of Hermann Rodriques. Eastern culture collides with Western culture to form a colourful depiction of today's Scots.

In Ragas & Reels, Bashabi Fraser consolidates her reputation as one of the foremost poets of contemporary Scotland. Her loyalties to both India and Scotland are deep and active... In this new collection of beautifully turned, carefully poised poems, she co-ordinates these loyalties of understanding and sympathy in ways which invite the reader to take fresh stock of her or his own position in a rapidly changing global economy, and to return to the things which are most deeply nourishing.
ALAN RIACH

[Hermann Rodriques'] work shows a vibrant cultural fusion, a two-way street with South Asian communities adapting to embrace Scottish traditions to construct a peculiarly Scottish-Asian way of life, as well as influencing the culture of their adopted home.
SCOTLAND NOW

From the Ganga to the Tay: A poetic conversation between the Ganges and the Tay

Bashabi Fraser
ISBN 978-1906307-95-0 PBK £8.99

The mythical qualities of Indian rivers is profound with daily rituals imprinted in community consciousness. Scotland's rivers were also recognised as the life blood of mother earth, and considered sacred, but cultural evolution seems to have clouded our ancestors' respect for Scotland's most powerful river, the Tay.
KENNY MUNRO

From the Ganga to the Tay is an epic poem in which the Indian River Ganges and the Scottish River Tay, the largest waterways in their countries, relate the historical importance of the ties between India and Scotland. The rivers are potent natural symbols of continuity and peace. With stunning photographs, the conversation between the rivers explores centuries of shared history between Scotland and India as well as each river's personal journey through time.

In the art of Bashabi Fraser the cultures of India and Scotland richly blend, and in this magnificent poem the two living traditions speak to each other through the riverine oracles of the Ganges and the Tay.
RICHARD HOLLOWAY

Tartan and Turban

Bashabi Fraser
ISBN 978-1-842820-44-5 PBK £8.99

Let the powder clouds of Holi – the festival of colour – cover you in purple, pink and green.

Be mesmerised by the proud hooded cobra weaving its charm.

Join a wedding wrapped up in reams of yellow silk and incense and alive with the swish of green kilts and the sound of bagpipes.

Watch the snow melt on the crest of soft dawns and feel the slash of rain against your numb cheek as the wind races across from the North Sea.

Read Bashabi Fraser's poetry and experience a swirl of emotions and images.

A Bengali poet living in Scotland, Bashabi Fraser creatively spans the different worlds she inhabits, celebrating the contrasts of the two countries whilst also finding commonality. Focusing on clear themes and issues – displacement, removal, belonging, identity, war – her poetry is vibrant with feeling and comes alive in an outrageous game of sound patterns.

... mixes up some extraordinarily tasty Indian rhythms with eloquent, Saltirephile verse.
THE LIST

Clocking In Clocking Out Poems and Photographs on the subject of Work

Brian Whittingham

ISBN 978-1-908373-17-5 PBK £8.99

When someone asks, 'What do you do?' you tend to define yourself by the job that you do or do not do – as society generally does. Sometimes it seems that your job is the sum total of all that you are.
BRIAN WHITTINGHAM

Whether you are a hairdresser or a hangman, a boxer or a bus driver, your job is your role in life which must be maintained. The poems in this collection touch on the universal experience of work and what it means to each of us. Are we defined by the job we do, or do we define the jobs we have?

Clocking In Clocking Out captures the full range of emotions that come from at least 40 years of clocking in and out, before we are eventually forced, one last time, to clock out.

Like [Walt] Whitman, Whittingham's poetry is not confined to the significance of his own workplaces, or to labourers of the past, but to the large phenomenon of labour as a window into the human character and condition.
DR SHARON CUMBERLAND, Director, Creative Writing Program, Seattle University

Bunnets n Bowlers: A Clydeside Odyssey

Brian Whittingham

ISBN 978-1906307-94-3 PBK £8.99

'Ach, bit thers nae need tae worry, ah'll get yi a joab in the yards, yi'll be fixed up fur life so yi wull, fixed up fir life'

Every ship has a story, and so does every shipbuilder, whether they are bowler hats, the foremen whose job it was to make sure deadlines were met, or bunnets, the skilled artisans that did the graft.

Meet the characters of The Black Squad: Sam Abbott, the knicker knocker from Duntocher; Wild Bill Hickok, the card shark; Irish Pat, the burner who likes his bevvy too much, and many more. They've spent their lives together in John Brown's shipyard sharing in the hilarity and tragedy of their work.

Brian Whittingham started his career in the Clydeside shipyards at just 15 years old when a job in the yards was for life. *Bunnets n Bowlers* follows this Clydeside odyssey, familiar to so many, from smart-arsed apprentice to skilled artisan and celebrates the humour and camaraderie of an ailing profession.

Earth

John Hudson
ISBN 978-1-908373-36-6 PBK £8.99

I, Earth, third rock from Sun,
hot stuff, fatal attraction,
Mister Magnetic,
surf gravity in a dicey embrace,
on a roll, a Salchow, wave-crest,
tumbling, never landing

I, Earth, the real 24/7/365,
say hello,
open my leafy hand,
my cavernous heart.

In *Earth*, John Hudson asks the perennial question: What does it mean to be human in an ever-changing world?

A collection of poems that takes the reader on a journey that explores the relationship, at times personal, at others social, mythical and philosophical, between humans and our planet, poems that address our past, our future, our dreams and nightmares, poems of welcome and farewell.

Scunnered: Slices of Scottish Life in Seventeen Gallus Syllables

Des Dillon
ISBN: 978 1 908373 01 4 PBK £7.99

A book to make you laugh. A book to make you cry. A book to make you rage against the injustices of the world. A book to make you feel better about it all. Perhaps. Perhaps not.

This is a collection of thoughts and ideas in Haiku on subjects including Science, Ecology, Nature, Family, Scotland, the Arts, Politics, Psychology, Philosophy, Spirituality and Love. Prepare to laugh, cry and wonder at this wonderful wee book of Haiku with a large slice of Scottish life.

Aristotle on Scotland
Nature produces
nothing without good reason;
save midges and neds.
Scunnered

Some more poetry from **LUATH** PRESS

The Luath Kilmarnock Edition: Poems Chiefly in the Scottish Dialect
Robert Burns
ISBN: 978-1-906307-67-7 HBK £15

Merry Muses of Caledonia
Robert Burns
ISBN: 978-1-906307-68-4 HBK £15

Dancing with Big Eunice
Alistair Findlay
ISBN: 978-1-906817-28-2 PBK £7.99

The Love Songs of John Knox
Alistair Findlay
ISBN: 978-1-905222-30-8 PBK £7.99

Never Mind the Captions
Alistair Findlay
ISBN: 978-1-906817-89-3 PBK £7.99

Shale Voices
Alistair Findlay
ISBN: 978-1-906307-11-0 PBK £10.99

Kate o Shanter's Tale
Matthew Fitt
ISBN: 978-1-842820-28-5 PBK £6.99

Jane: Poems of a Performance Poet
Anita Govan
ISBN: 978-1-905222-14-8 PBK £6.99

Blind Ossian's Fingal
James Macpherson
ISBN: 978-1-906817-55-8 HBK £15

Love and Revolution
Alastair Mcintosh
ISBN: 978-1-905222-58-2 PBK £8.99

Burning Whins
Liz Niven
ISBN: 978-1-842820-74-2 PBK £8.99

Stravaigin
Liz Niven
ISBN: 978-1-905222-70-4 PBK £7.99

Bad Ass Raindrop
Kokumo Rocks
ISBN: 978-1-842820-18-6 PBK £6.99

Stolen from Africa
Kokumo Rocks
ISBN: 978-1-906307-19-6 PBK £7.99

Bodywork
Dilys Rose
ISBN: 978-1-905222-93-3 PBK £8.99

A Long Stride Shortens the Road
Donald Smith
ISBN: 978-1-842820-73-5 PBK £8.99

Into the Blue Wavelengths
Roderick Watson
ISBN: 978-1-842820-75-9 PBK £8.99

Drink the Green Fairy
Brian Whittingham
ISBN: 978-1-842820-45-2 PBK £8.99

Accent o the Mind
Rab Wilson
ISBN: 978-1-905222-32-2 PBK £8.99

Life Sentence
Rab Wilson
ISBN: 978-1-906307-89-9 PBK £8.99

A Map for the Blind
Rab Wilson
ISBN: 978-1-906817-82-4 PBK £8.99

The Ruba'iyat of Omar Kayyam in Scots
Rab Wilson
ISBN: 978-1-842820-46-9 PBK £8.99

Details of these and other books published by Luath Press can be found at:
www.luath.co.uk

Luath Press Limited

committed to publishing well written books worth reading

LUATH PRESS takes its name from Robert Burns, whose little collie Luath (*Gael.*, swift or nimble) tripped up Jean Armour at a wedding and gave him the chance to speak to the woman who was to be his wife and the abiding love of his life. Burns called one of 'The Twa Dogs' Luath after Cuchullin's hunting dog in Ossian's *Fingal*. Luath Press was established in 1981 in the heart of Burns country, and now resides a few steps up the road from Burns' first lodgings on Edinburgh's Royal Mile.

Luath offers you distinctive writing with a hint of unexpected pleasures.

Most bookshops in the UK, the US, Canada, Australia, New Zealand and parts of Europe either carry our books in stock or can order them for you. To order direct from us, please send a £sterling cheque, postal order, international money order or your credit card details (number, address of cardholder and expiry date) to us at the address below. Please add post and packing as follows: UK – £1.00 per delivery address; overseas surface mail – £2.50 per delivery address; overseas airmail – £3.50 for the first book to each delivery address, plus £1.00 for each additional book by airmail to the same address. If your order is a gift, we will happily enclose your card or message at no extra charge.

Luath Press Limited
543/2 Castlehill
The Royal Mile
Edinburgh EH1 2ND
Scotland
Telephone: 0131 225 4326 (24 hours)
Fax: 0131 225 4324
email: sales@luath.co.uk
Website: www.luath.co.uk

Printed by RR Donnelley at Glasgow, UK